For Greg—
Best of luck i[n]
Poetry & all [...]
swirling about [...]
Chaos

CHAOS THEORY

Christopher Buckley

Christopher Buckley

a plume editions book

AN IMPRINT OF MadHat Press

Asheville, North Carolina

MadHat Press
MadHat Incorporated
PO Box 8364, Asheville, NC 28814

The Library of Congress has assigned
this edition a Control Number of
2017910060

ISBN 978-1-941196-53-3 (paperback)

Text by Christopher Buckley
Cover image by Marc Vincenz
Cover design by Marc Vincenz

Plume Editions
an imprint of MadHat Press
www.MadHat-Press.com

First Printing

TABLE OF CONTENTS

I. CHAOS THEORY:

II.

III.

He looked at his own Soul
with a Telescope. What Seemed
all irregular, he saw and
shewed to be beautiful
Constellations; and he added
to the Consciousness hidden
worlds within worlds.
—COLERIDGE, *Notebooks*

I say unto you: one must still have chaos in oneself
to be able to give birth to a dancing star. I say unto you:
you still have chaos in yourselves.
—NIETZSCHE

After your death you will be what you were before your birth.
—SCHOPENHAUER

second star to the right, and straight on till morning
—J.M. BARRIE

I. Chaos Theory

I. Chaos Theory

The systems that the theory describes are apparently disordered, but Chaos Theory is really about finding the underlying order in apparently random data.
      —https://courses.seas.harvard.edu/climate/eli/Courses/
EPS281r/Sources/Chaos-and-weather-prediction/1-Chaos-Theory-A-
Brief-Introduction-IMHO.pdf

there is no such thing
as no such thing
      —Dennis Saleh

3.3 billion years ago we caught a break ...
      bacteria on a meteor falling
from the far side of nowhere splashed down
      and this cosmic ham-bone
converted our atmosphere to one with oxygen
      from one without—all it would be
our good fortune to breathe as we eventually
      crawled out from under
the rocks and sat around beneath banana palms
      and birds of paradise
formulating philosophies about the origins of beauty,
      why there is something
instead of nothing, if there is any meaning
      in meaning, and how unlikely it is
that anyone will ever bat over .400 again....
      Even post-Eden, the trees
seemed organized and cooperative as we
      gathered things, looked up, and,
in a range of voices over un-swept savannahs,
      praised and gave thanks beneath
the unstained light of the Corona Borealis
      for Beaujolais and stock

3

derivatives, stars falling every which way
    across the old hangar dome
of Pangaea—industrial revolution, gold,
    and dust beyond our dreams.

Thrown in as a bonus, the invisible glitter-bits
    in the electromagnetic spectrum
unabsorbed and concentrated in the ionosphere,
    reflecting radiation back into space—
and, we only recently realized, an ozone layer
    on a limited-time offer,
absorbing ultraviolet—Thank You very much—
    without which we'd fry like fish
cakes in a skillet, and not one lima bean, lentil,
    or loquat would grow; so hot,
unbeknownst to us, that the planet would lose all
    its water the way Mars did early on,
before we had a snowball's proverbial chance.
    What luck. As far as it goes,
as long as it lasts. That first astrolabe carved
    from shoulder blades, gauging
our tangential interest in and long-distance relevance to
    the stars, did not divulge
the scaffoldings and strategies, the dimensions at work
    all about and beneath us.
We were happy, filled in the blanks with good intentions,
    our observations fashioned
largely in the dark, our lungs, working from the bottom up
    as we decided we had something
to prove. We selected a god, some gods—answers
    weren't as hard to come by

as iron and fire. But it seemed a reasonable place to start
    before the continents began
to split apart and we surfed out on the back of time's
    white and unseen scroll, before
the fellows in Athens began to formulate atomic hypotheses
    and the various reified situations
of the air that would lead us eventually to the unknotted
    tangles of string theory and eleven
dimensions, parallel universes and the probable impossible
    grab bag and jumble of everything.

II. 1959

1959's as good example as any: 6th grade with transistor radios
    and "Shimmy Shimmy Ko-Ko Bop"
by Little Anthony & The Imperials is a hit with its 12/8 time
       signature,
    the group never acknowledging the influence
of Wallace Stevens, whose theme of universal fluctuation
    is a constant throughout his work.
And, pulling 10¢ from my pocket to pay for a Milky Way,
    I had no idea that it was Stevens' wife,
Elsie, who posed for sculptor Adolph A. Weinman—
    from whom they rented a NYC apartment—
and whose profile he used for the design of the Mercury dime.

    And Santo & Johnny's "Sleep Walk"
with its slurry twang climbs the charts to #1 that September—
    the birds lazy in the arms of the air,
every note drifting past my weak hold on the clouds
    back there, and in Louisville,
my grandfather's heart imploding like a red star....
    A single engine plane in the light
over the stilled metropolis, mail bags dropping
    into Sioux Falls in a timely manner
in our Social Studies text, and no one looking up.
    I'll have no idea who she is
for another dozen years, but Billie Holliday
    will die desperately in February,
and Cecil B. De Mille and Frank Lloyd Wright as well.
    Castro will run Fulgencio Batista
and his big U.S. investors out of Cuba on January 2nd,
    and the men in Switzerland
will vote against voting rights for women. Japanese-

Americans will regain citizenship,
Nikita Khrushchev be denied access to Disneyland.
        Pioneer IV sends radio signals
400,000 miles to earth, where Groucho, Harpo & Chico appear
        together on TV for the last time.
Gen. Charles de Gaulle is inaugurated as president of France,
        the Dalai Lama flees Tibet
for India. Oklahoma ends prohibition after 51 years.
        Alex Olmeda beats Rod Laver
at Wimbledon in 71 minutes, and Harvey Haddix pitches
        12 perfect innings and loses in the 13th.
Congress authorizes Food Stamps for poor Americans,
        a tamale, rice and beans are $1.25
at Tiny's on Milpas St. in Santa Barbara where I saw
        Davy Crockett (Fess Parker)
when I was 9. The Postmaster General bans Lawrence's
        Lady Chatterley's Lover, and
on July 24th the 500,000th Dutch TV set is registered.
        Ford cancels production of the Edsel.
Jack Benny (violin) and Richard Nixon (piano) play
        their famed duet in black & white.
A pair to draw to, nothing wild. It's all in the mix—
        you can't make this stuff up.

III. The Universal Law of Impermanence

Anything produced by causes is susceptible to change....
—the Dalai Lama, *The Universe In A Single Atom*

When the bell rang each day
at 3:00, I was always happy
to put away the science reports,
the exercises I was working on

in longhand across the extended horizon
of our copy books, and race out
to the playing field where nothing
had happened all afternoon without us

except for the re-positioning of air,
the photosynthesis of grass and acacia leaves,
the bright, invisible starlight showering
down. The new standard model holds

that only 4% of the universe is composed
of atoms—a wholesale shift from all
the certainties only a few years back,
and no matter how many striped stones

we pick up on the beach, nothing
is going to keep us permanently in place
beside the sea. Even if we learned
the absolute facts about space and time,

in these bodies, could we live our lives
any differently? *Dalai Lama* means
"Ocean Guru," signifying an ocean
of compassion. But looking out

at the heaven's flung net, it's unlikely
there is anything that will allow us
to escape the stars with our pocketfuls
of dust ... dust the wind's only banner.

Like the wind, like the dust, I have
never had the least desire to join
anything, especially organized systems
of belief. It seems true that no one

in charge really thinks of us, and
it's never taken much to erect
a slipshod monument to one theory
or another from our dutiful bones.

Any conditional absolute tells us,
Yes, probably, in most cases ... light
and matter dissipate, or add up—just
not necessarily to us, every time.

IV. Stuff Happens

At the Large Hadron Collider
                        outside Geneva,
the conventions of existence
                   are breaking
                         down …
if the theory of a
            mathematically precise universe
                            obtains,
then we would never exist.
                   Relativity
                     and quantum mechanics
both tell us
          that equal amounts
                  of matter and anti-
                         matter
should have appeared
             with the Big Bang,
                   and instantly
canceled each other out—
                 no side effects, no residual
background radiation,
             not one note of celestial Muzak.
There shouldn't be
           a single stellar grease spot
                      or cosmic sub-
atomic stain,
         no dark invisible
                matter or energy,
                   not the thinnest
smoky whisper
         to tickle

God's deaf ear.

But at Fermilab,

the DZero team

is coming up

with neutral B-mesons—

particles

famous for not being

able to make up their minds,

oscillating

trillions of times a second,

back and forth between matter

and

anti-matter.... In fireball particle collisions

they go from

an antimatter state

to a matter state

faster than

the other way

around, leaving more matter

when they decay

to *muons*—fat electrons,

essentially—tilting the machine, if you will,

for a throw-back replay,

the payoff being 1% more matter

left on the plate

in that reconstituted

universe of particles

pin-balling

inside the collider.

I go back

11

to 5th grade,
   problems with the dividend
      and divisor, long division,
the vague work toward a quotient.
     I never knew if there'd be
something left over
    after I'd carried over the whole numbers
through the variables
    happening hour by hour
      at the invisible
speed of light.
   I stood out
    in the school yard
      looking up, sun-blind
after the bell rang
   wondering
    what exactly was being divided
into what all around me,
    and what
     mathematical disparity,
infinitesimal cosmic slip-up and quantum
      sleight of hand,
would, in theory, or in fact,
    account for us
      when the dust settled.

V. Prime Mover vs. Qualitative Nonlinear Differential Equations

(* a found poem)

Differential equations are used to describe the change
    or quantities of behavior

of certain systems. Analytical solutions cannot, in general,
    be found—cannot be written out.

We may make numerical approximations, however in most
    applications solutions may be

unavailable. People are interested in questions such as:
    Will the system have at least one

solution? Will the system have at most one solution?
    It is also beneficial to learn

how to analyze the existence and uniqueness of systems—
    stability, chaos, and boundedness.

Before a numerical approximation is carried out, the existence
    and uniqueness of solutions should be

checked to make sure that there does exist one and only one
    solution. Otherwise, how does one know

what one is approximating? Even though numerical solutions
    suggest certain properties,

they are only valid for limited solutions on finite intervals,
    and therefore cannot be

used to determine the qualitative properties of all solutions
to the original equation.

VI. Nothing

You know what you can do with it—
the body when the spirit's drained,
when the ashes are returned....
Divide by air, by earth, carry
the bones ... no remainder, nothing
left over; not even the next to nothing
that was there to start with,
just the loose change of the dark
that counts for nothing.
                   The universe
doesn't add up. Only 4% of everything
is actually something, actually matter
that matters, shining for all it's worth.
These are the percentages we play, the hope
we hang our metaphysical hats on,
any belief of being re-circulated
in light. We wouldn't know the invisible
all around us even if it were there—
wherever there is?
                No second chances,
no do-overs. When it's all said and done,
it's all said and done. We know
from nothing. It's all or nothing, or all
then nothing—it's to be, or not....
It's nothing to laugh at, good for nothing,
nothing but trouble. There's nothing
further from the truth—there's something
to try and get your mind around
before you have nothing left
to think with. Has it all been for nothing—

this law of diminishing
returns?
        If you get small—subatomic—
all of Einstein's laws are a bust,
a bunch of probability outcomes,
absolute uncertainty that zeros-out
the accounts—0 and 00 on the wheel
to skew the odds so the house takes it all.
Our pockets emptied, biologically speaking,
or otherwise. But it's nothing
you can put your finger on....

Erase the blackboard, clap the erasers,
and there we are, white chalk
dissipating in no time, into cosmic
long division, the algebra where
you cannot solve for x, where nothing
stands for itself or anything else
for long … a place where all the time
has gone like lost breath …
no place holders, not a single scintilla
of everlasting anything. No nothing,
come to no good, and thanks
for nothing.
        Aristotle, like nature,
hated a void. He had probable cause,
as he saw the stars sledded back
and forth by angels on crystal tracks
around the earth. Now cosmologists
say everything came from nothing—
primordial nothing, blank soupless soup,

then matter and antimatter until
something slips up and shakes
that balance, elbowing out
an uneven contingent of muons,
of neutrinos, ghost particles
of decay carrying away
energy—the process, they say,
which ignites stars, gives us
light with all subsequent properties
and forces of space and time expanding,
and by and by we swim out
from the mix, breathe and
start from scratch, relishing
this sweet nothing, it's all
ex nihilo, as the Romans had it.
No matter what, it looks like
we are left with naught,
nada, nugatory, goose eggs, zilch,
zip, gaps, vacuums, diddly-squat
and a cosmos of bugger-all
coming out in the wash.
How many parts per zillion,
our atoms diluted to nothing?
Best to ignore the stars
though they might be everything
there is by way of temporary
reference.
   The universe then
as crème brulée, our gauzy galaxy
an improbable confection of star-floss
spiraling around the center,

the egg yolk whirling against the dark
drift of space, like a dervish
hoping to achieve ecstasy,
rotating under the dome of heaven.
Though everything is done
under the aspect of eternity,
and every star is devout
in its hymn of light.
The equations may or may not
elegantly resolve … either way,
at the very least, it's a crapshoot
from the get-go, and back
to stardust for us all.
Here goes nothing.…

VII. Fractals

Every great and deep difficulty bears in itself its own solution.
It forces us to change our thinking in order to find it.
        —Niels Bohr

A coastline, if measured down to its least irregularity,
tends toward infinite length, as do snow flakes. Clouds
or coastlines, no matter how close or far away we get,
the basic pattern, the surface and volume, repeat
ad infinitum....
                    Cloud or cauliflower, rough, broken
geometric shapes have an area that is finite, but
a perimeter that is not.
                    It's a short walk from there
to Thomas Aquinas and Co., First Cause and effect,
and an intellectual trail of consecrated bread crumbs
back to a source we reflect.
                    Computers came along
and we can enumerate all the patterned variations
in nature—lightning bolts, river networks, broccoli,
the branching of the circulatory system, pine cones
and ferns.
                    Right now, someone is calculating the connection
between fractals and leaves in order to estimate how much
CO_2 there is in trees, to help the environment with carbon
emission control so we might go on breathing and
piecing things together.
                    Jackson Pollock's paintings
appear to be composed of chaotic drippings and splatters,
but computers have mapped recursive patterns in the work;
high voltage has been trapped in an acrylic block, repeating
the bronchial patterns of trees.

19

                    Star clusters form
paisley patterns, and patterns repeat in the wobbly
orbits of satellites in the solar system, in weather,
economics, earthquakes and plate tectonics, and in
the mathematical model of eye-tracking disorders
among schizophrenics.
                    Our universe could be a bubble
on an ocean of bubbles; a nearby universe might have Al Gore
as president and Elvis still singing in Las Vegas?
                                        Just like
the currents of the ocean, the brain itself might be organized
according to the laws of chaos—enfolded labyrinths, invisible
synaptic lingua franca, its grey death-mask mosaic
of temporary matter, the incremental and incidental tiles,
fragments that replicate, accumulate, and account for us
in every particular, and then are dispersed into the burning
dust fusing into the stars, into the silence that fills
every unaccounted for corner of the dark.

VIII. Time Out

One can think of the universe as being like a giant casino,
with dice rolled or wheels being spun on every occasion.
—Stephen Hawking

Salt air, sun glitter along the cliff—they could represent
      anything now. The eucalyptus,
trees of my childhood, are shaking their heads—
      something I have
or haven't done.... Who's to blame—everything green
      long gone in my bones?
Finally, it's almost enough to smell the honeysuckle
      and pittosporum, the sweet
fragrance of grease from the burger joints in 1964
      riding that air along State Street,
another mid-January hot spell, all the windows down
      in that boat of a '59 Bel Air.
Clouds scattered like rose petals thrown on holy days
      down the center aisle
of the church by girls in white taffeta.... Time Out!
      King's X! as we called, midway
in a game of freeze-tag or kick-ball, suspending the rules,
      catching our breath,
thinking we could halt the insensate spin of the globe,
      the ball mid-air, the blood-burn
in our cheeks, the carousel of every invisible particle
      that we had no idea made us up,
the ongoing wager of our flesh holding together ever-after,
      and not wandering off in a field
of light, or darkness, like the evenings we hoped
      would linger as we ran through
them for all that we were worth. Now all bets are off,

too late to double down,
to recoup our losses, not a chance in hell for a last-minute
        starry five-card-Charlie
consecrated wild-card-cash-in as they add more decks
        to the shoe and you lose
count of the face cards and where you ever were
        in the system. Time and matter
were just the ante; now they've worked out an equation
        for the game with an infinite
number of strings attached. The wheel spins faster,
        no catechism or super computer
big enough to tote up the likely possibilities for
        any good they might do you.
We are all time travelers, shot relentlessly forward.
        From here it looks like the soul
takes the form of sea foam and washes away,
        up in to the air, for as long
as you have the cosmic wherewithal, for as long
        as you have the time.

IX. Chaos Thinking

Nadya asks,
   Are you asleep, or just lying there
           thinking
about the universe again?
      Nothing much resolved
since the last time,
    I say....
      I'm going over String Theory
—multiverses, 11 dimensions—
       the books tell me
that strings
    account for all matter,
       that they're pure
geometry,
   and not really made up of anything?
         (Plato was sure
that God was the Super Geometer—
       the unintended irony.)
I was also reading that the 3
    (or 4)
      dimensions we live in
probably evolved
    from 9 or 10
      in the early universe,
rendering us
   the leaner, trimmed-down,
       competitive models
of carbon-based life.
    But a lot of the space
      in my bed
is taken up

by my cat, Cecil B
and his grey spiral galaxy of fur ...
his big sleepy head on my arm
as the gears and flywheels
of the night
whir out there
above us.

It takes
almost as many
types of molecules
to make an apricot
as it does a person.
If you look closely,
get down
to mesons,
assorted unseen
bits and pieces,
there's not so much difference
between Cecil and myself
except that I received a larger serving,
and with it more capacity
for untethered thought
about the stardust
that backfills the blueprints
of our bodies,
while he takes more
for granted,
although he is as anxious about
what's in the garden
and on the other side of the street

as I am
about the other side
of the river....

Now they really do see
how everything came from nothing,
but I have to wonder
where we got nothing from?
The sun
is a big clock,
its spots appearing in eleven-year cycles,
the whole thing
pulsing in regular 5-minute intervals—
where would we be
without the sun;
who is minding the clocks?
Neither my cat nor I
are gamblers—
we like our meals on time.
Cecil stretches out
saying
anything you can do in 4 dimensions
I'm already doing in 3—
who needs 11?
We all could use more
gravy on our plates.
Newton was sure space was filled with
a luminous ether
that transported waves of light
the way air carries
waves of sound.

Now it seems nothing
in the fullness of time
is full.
Entropy keeps us all moving
in one direction,
toward
the literal and allegorical dark,
though astronomers
at Johns Hopkins
have determined that the universe is beige.
The human brain
is hard-wired to perceive
patterns in random events—
we'd like,
while we have a chance,
to make some sense of our surroundings—
The Sacred Heart of Jesus
burned into a tortilla,
Einstein's face
floating in the clouds ...
we take a moment to compare
the beaks
of Darwin's finches
to the stars, the relative time taken
to evolve ...
And after it works
through us and escapes,
light has to be
headed somewhere....
Anything we touched
and held onto in the first place,

is gone
once we've turned it over
a time or two,
in our minds.

X. In Memory of Air

Between here and the sky, the egg-shell
edge of the ionosphere, the indistinct

eons of rising mist. Any memory of life
and death and life again, any clue

regarding destinations after the fact—
superstring arithmetics, additional

soap-bubble universes—distorts like light
bent around a star in the jumbled serape

of the cosmos, far beyond anywhere
we're ever going, no matter how fast

the capsule or how long we hold our breath.
We might as well question the clouds.

      *   *   *

Nitrogen, oxygen, and water vapor—
molecular cocktail we take in entirely

on faith; half of our air thins into auroras,
the muddled edge of space. Below,

in the upper layers, "air glow"—
sheets of photons emitting a blue

both visible and invisible to our eyes.
This is our 3rd and last atmosphere.

The first burnt off; the second simmered
away, all CO_2 and volcanic ammonia.

Then bacteria turned up, converting it all
so we might crawl out from under the sea.

      *   *   *

The bituminous night, and God beyond
the stratosphere, discontent from the get-go.

So what in the world preserves the tongue
of St. Anthony mounted on a rusted spike,

what keeps the atmosphere that strips us
down over time, away? What element

sustains each voice-print, each atom
of alleluia or rebuke for our bread

and circuses, for self denial in the name
of anything in back of the blue?

      *   *   *

My skydiving days are over....
Older, I am less and less certain

of what might sustain a little kite
of faith? Always, stars have been dying

above the wind. The Milky Way
reflects our thirst for the infinite—

29

bright gasp, aqueduct of light, all
of us designed with death in mind.

With the next cloud passing, the longing
of the waves, we might agree then—

everything is worth our attention.
On the sea cliff, in a gale, my arms embrace

all that time has come to—held briefly
in the circuitry of the blood, at my fingertips.

What hair I have is the color of clouds.
When I am ash, will I be faithful to the earth

or the aether? Where will I go to find myself
again, set down like a dry seed by wind?

*　　*　　*

Before the vacant horizon, it's easy
to remember God—I have to hope

there is something. The upper regions,
oblique as the far edge of Eden, are dulled

with molecules our lungs first took in,
longing for land beneath us, the azure

chemicals of heaven randomly calculated
above. I can sit on my bench and wonder

from where bacteria, 3.3 billion years ago,
arrived so we might breathe and walk about

as if we knew what we were doing here.
My atoms will outlive me, recombining

to fill the troposphere, too late to save
the earth—the galvanized seas then,

the last emblems of our indifference.
I'm just another one inhaling the un-

enduring sky, entered in the raffle of clouds,
passing through a last blue gate of air.

XI. God Particle

17. If God is everywhere, why do we not see Him?
        —(Lesson 2, "God and His Perfections," from the *Baltimore Catechism*

So I would not say that this announcement is the equivalent of seeing the face of God, but it might turn out to be the toe of God.
        —Joe Lykken, theorist at Fermilab, on the Higgs boson being possibly detected.

In the popular media, the particle is sometimes referred to as the God Particle, a title generally disliked by the scientific community as media hyperbole that misleads readers.
—Wikipedia

First grade put an end to ontology,
                        to any necessity for scientific enquiry
with Lesson 1 in the *Baltimore Catechism*,
                        "The Purpose of Man's Existence:"
1. Who made us? God Made us.
                2. Who is God? God is the Supreme Being,
infinitely perfect, who made all things,
                and keeps them in existence.

We drove along the coast
                with the top down,
                        lemon blossoms lifting
to the stars....
                but a lifetime later,
                        there is nothing,
                                for all appearances,
out there
        holding us
                together,

nothing holding us
in place—
just a bright scattering
of dusts
every time
we look into the great
blind degree of night
with only a grab bag of math
underwriting the dark
matter, or
dark energy, that binds
the galaxy's mystic spiral,
the intangible
reiteration—
stuff unlike anything
else we know
that seems
to be
working well enough
silently behind the scenes.

Yet the lab boys with their heads
under the cosmological hood,
with red-shifted
galactic grease rags
stuffed in their back pockets
tell us that
for the unified engine to work,
for the sub-atomic nuts
and bolts to click,
the fundamental force-

                                        carrying particles
must have mass,
                    contrary to theory and the scree of math.
You solve for X,
                    but the answer is not
                                        always X.
                                            It's back to
body and soul again,
                        the standard model
                                        of how the universe works,
or almost works,
                        coming up short
                                    when it comes to mass, to some
water in the conceptual bucket.
                                Mass describes how much
                                                    matter
a particle, molecule, or a cheese soufflé contains.
                                            Without mass,
particles, atoms, soufflés, and '59 Chevrolets
                                            would whip
recklessly about at the speed of light,
                                    disastrous for
the lemon blossoms
                    and clumps of matter
                                    we've become....
Higgs filled in the theoretical
                        blank
                            with an invisible force field
from the Big Bang,
                    a crucial boson
                                imparting mass to particles

as they pass through ...
                              (picture the space
                                        between God's finger
and Adam's as He gives life to Adam)....
                                        It's like walking through
snow, they say, collecting flakes on
                              your grey coat....
The Higgs boson definitively existed
                              in the minds
                                        of physicists,
but had not been not found
                              or excluded beyond doubt;
and Blaise Pascal came to mind again—
                              flipping a coin,
                                        his calculated
wagers in favor of God.
                     Today, in Switzerland, they are 99% certain
that they've turned it up—
                     one chance in a million,
                                        says the news release,
that it's a statistical fluke.
                     The new particle
                              has the predicted mass
for the boson,
          and behaves
                     as they think
                              the God Particle should
in accordance with its role
                     in the creation
                              and maintenance
of the universe.

35

Math or metaphysics,
                    quantum mechanics,
no matter how
          many parts describing the dual
                              particle or wave-like
interactions of energy and matter,
                    the final questions are the same:
scientist or saint,
          what can you put your finger on,
                              slip into
your transcendental bag—
                    the reliquary of the earth and its shining
atmosphere?
          What bit of anything is left over,
                              given what, if anything,
you started with—
          here and gone in a split second—
                              relative to
the rocks of time?
          We're left holding little more than
                              a dot-to-dot
terrestrial playbook,
          loose schematics
                    cut from infinitesimal grains
of cause and varying effects
                    hovering above the orchard....
In back of that,
          an equation intended
                    to explain everything
that arrived from nothing,
          that puts us on patrol

for a prime particle,
seen or not,
and by extension
a divine electromagnetic DNA—
theory stringing us together,
assuring us
of ourselves,
of life
everlasting
despite the sea in shambles,
despite the mute hymn
of every shooting star....

God-Particle Postscript from the Large Hadron Collider

Whereas we once believed,
                we now know—
                                at the LHC,
they have finally managed
                    to track the stray bits
                              and left-overs
of the photons
                    in that intelligently designed head-on crash …
and they confirm the invisible
                        background that effects
the way waves propagate—
                    (the packets of light Einstein saw
flip-flopping through an amorphous veil
                          and generating masses,
and mass differences
                in other elementary particles)
and thus the Higgs Boson,
                    endowing all matter with mass....

It's just a shade
            over the line
                  that makes up the vacuum—
the lowest energy state
                where there are no particles, but where
there's something....
              Elementary bits
                    (leptons and quarks)
that constitute all matter
              are *fermions;*
                    whereas *bosons*—
such as the God Particle—

are force-carriers,

the "glue"

holding all the bits together—

present everywhere

there's something there.

And if this sounds slightly familiar—

(massless,

out of nothing,

giving mass to matter

so that

the rest of everything

will not be nothing)—

no shred of evidence

has yet emerged

suggesting that photons have

even the slightest

religious inclination....

And now a new collider team

is challenging the single God-

Particle observation,

proposing that

the Higgs is 5 different particles in one—

same mass,

different charges—

a small statistical result

that nonetheless

amounts to more

than when you crank up

all the previous whirligigs

and gears,

                readouts and
unraveled representations in dust
                 to get at the mystery
a little more,
        prying another theoretical fingernail
beneath the dark,
          under the locked
                cabinet of the void,
into the harmony,
        and illusion of the universe.

II

Creed

I believe in dust,
the particle almighty,
every indestructible bit
of the heavens
and earth....
And in the icy breath
of comets, long shot
and fat chance
chaos of the quick
and the dead
burning down to us
with bacteria,
with mitochondrial DNA,
their scrawl engrained
on the clipboard
of the void,
silver stitches
across the night, the trace
elements of the infinite
dissolving,
first and last
emblems of the emptiness
where they streaked
from nothing
and were lost,
flying low
by the floorboards
of time, sliding
down the invisible
sluiceways of dark
energy which looks now

Christopher Buckley

like almost all of it,
whatever it is….
Neutrinos know us
for the loose assemblies
of dust we are,
and I have no choice
but to believe
that they do indeed
pass through us
as easily as God's thoughts.
And I believe blindly
in quarks, charmed
and strange, the unitary
negative charge of muons,
the impact carried
by gauge bosons,
the communion,
the constituent scaffolding
from which we're made—
and thus the cathedral
of the atom, every particle
and untied force
in the unified field
cast out and unforgiven
as gravity, holding us
here in the brief
embrace of our cells—
in eleven dimensions
undiscovered save for
some caliginous equations,
and in un-seeable strings

and every parallel membrane,
all which will be
resurrected in one star-
blast or another,
and stars only
4% of light everlasting
in its packets
and in its waves,
in the un-sourced
source, the unknown
and approximate shores
far from where we live.
I believe in the beginning
and the end, the near
or the far edge of space …
and whatever is
on the other side.

Online Facts About the Sun

Most of the time,
                I'm walking around
                                tossing ideas back and
forth with myself,
                waiting for a hollyhock,
                                the spice finches
who have just moved north,
                                or perhaps an eccentric cloud,
to suggest another way
                to look at things,
                                to stir the grey cells
a bit
        like a dust devil in the vacant lot....

                                But this morning
I read that photons from the surface of the sun
                                take 8 minutes
& 20 seconds
                to reach us and push back the dark—
which we don't see anyway—
                                and so I stopped and looked
out there wondering
                what in the world
                                our lives have come to,
given that at best, we're only a sustained blink
                                against oblivion?
And how many of us
                can do the math:
                                our orbit is 93 million,
205 thousand, 678 miles and change
                                away from the sun,

give or take a little wobbling,

which I'm more or less used to

being a citizen of a certain age....

And light moves at

186,282 miles per second,

which comes out to 8 minutes & 20

seconds

for the one-way trip

to get photosynthesis going

or burn

our skin on the beach....

More intriguing

is the journey

of photons in the sun's core

beginning as gamma radiation,

emitted,

then re-absorbed, in the radiative zone;

they wander

around

in there for tens of thousand of years before

they escape

to arrive on my patio.

So, as we look out, or up

into space,

into sunlight for a second,

we're actually looking back in time,

the way astronomers

tuning in the blue glow

of quasars

are looking back

some 14 billion years....

And, 83 million
light-years away
in galaxy M109, if aliens
are at their telescopes
dialing our planet in, they're watching
brontosauruses grazing
the tree tops,
triceratops lumbering along,
and are nowhere close
to deducing
that we'll eventually show up
and turn it all around
with our industrial revolution
and never-ending carbon emissions ...
Even the light
from your computer is nanoseconds old, and
moonlight, no matter how much
romantic cargo it carries,
takes only a second to reflect
to the surface of the sea....

The sun makes up
99.8% of the mass of the solar system and most
of the rest of it is Jupiter,
which makes us small potatoes indeed.
Like the earth, the sun is slowly heating up,
but it has no choice
given its atomic fusion;
we keep burning coal and oil
and looking
for our stock dividends.

The sun is mainly hydrogen
                          and helium,
and every billion years it is 10% more luminous—
                             eventually
there will be no water on earth
                to grow those potatoes.

Still, time and light
            are worth considering,
                        especially when
you are running short of both
                and there is limited availability
to look into the past and apply
                any worthwhile lessons
with lasting effect.

Anthropic Principle

In astrophysics and cosmology, the anthropic principle is the philosophical consideration that observations of the physical Universe must be compatible with the conscious life that observes it.

The most you can do is walk against the wind and clouds,
And sometimes return to a place from which you've come.
                    —Amichai

No wonder.

It all looks infinite enough....

Zero in on a few clusters
in the night sky, burning
out there like beach fires,
and they suggest a shore somewhere
at the other side of wherever
it was we started making metaphors,
wherever we began sailing
toward an indefinable
light, staring up.... Soon,
it all looked exactly like
what we expected it would
as we did little more than
circumnavigate our hopes
and suppositions—where else
were we really going?
                    Everything
we think up—given our parochial
vantage point—glitters for a while,
even though it's likely
there is more dark

on the far side of the dark.
                              True enough,
each night the Milky Way empties
into the heavens like a stream spun out
above the earth's misted breath,
into a place where time might dissolve
like water glittering into air,
or darkness—
                  an easy bridge
from there back down to the ancients
living in clouds, or in the shelves
of the sea—as good a chance
as not that there have been no gods
beyond these.
                  For every particle
in the universe today, there was
a precursor particle, existing
from the beginning
and no explanation of where
it came from—sounds like science
a little too cozy with faith?
As a kid, whenever I tried
one version or another of that
line of thinking—explaining
how I'd lost my milk money,
or how the green beans
on my plate disappeared
only to turn up later in my pocket—
I didn't meet with much success.

Who submitted the blueprints
for carbon 14, for the triple-
alpha process with 6 protons,
6 neutrons and 6 electrons
created in stars, for sea water
the antecedent of our blood?
Doesn't it sound like guesswork
in the wind? Clouds are best
compared to clouds,
no matter what we might
make of them....
              And each one
of our protons is composed
of three *quarks—up, up, and down—*
as well as *gluons*, and transitory pairs
of *sea quarks.* They think they're sure
now how every least bit
of life breaks down in the rush
and swim of things,
and almost no mass....
This afternoon however,
the leaves of the sycamore
look heavier. I think there is more
melancholy than irony in the trees—
but it could just be age....
             The wind
lays down and the sky surrenders
every iota of color, and it seems now
that time is catching up with us,
if, that is, you believe time
is doing anything at all....

Either way, it's too late to enunciate
the obvious or we would not be
sad, confused, transformed
by each reluctance, each swirl
of dust in the evening light
as we look out from the porch—
the night rising behind the stars
deep and blue as doubt
as far as we can see ...
like we knew it always would.

The Half-life of Revolution—Particle Physics, History, Baseball, & Baby-Boomers

> *Half-life … is typically used to describe a property of radioactive decay, but may be used to describe any quantity which follows an exponential decay.*
> —Wikipedia

So far, the information
                          is that quarks and leptons make up matter,
photons are mass-less,
                          neutrinos jump around
                                    like fleas on a dog—
yet every last bit arrived here out of the same blast …
                                    all of us then lucky
leftovers, though
                          our particles are petering out
                                    from the get-go….
Same difference no matter how
                          we record or interpret our actions,
our dissipation—
                          every last atom ticking
                                    steadily away before being
reallocated to the circuitry of the stars.

            *   *   *

A few years back, radical Islamists in Egypt joined secularists to oust Mubarak, then the Muslims took over with a front man in a Western suit and tie, who promised rights for all—a democratic split—who never delivered, who legislated and strong-armed in their own theocratic favor. Now, the military is back, more blood in the streets—no change. Orwell wrote a book….

            *   *   *

Sima Qian, the first,
             and some say greatest historian, said
the purpose of history was to teach
                   rulers how to govern well,
not to record how men die.
               Convicted of treason, he was castrated
instead of being executed
             for supporting the honor and loyal record
of a defeated general.

       *   *   *

"History is totally political in China, and I think it always has been,"
writes Frances Wood, historian and authority on China. They pick
and mix, editing and inventing facts. In the Great Museum in Beijing,
you hear about 1964's first nuclear test, the great reform era after
Mao's death, and not one syllable about tens of millions who died in
Mao's Great Leap Forward or in the Cultural Revolution.

       *   *   *

Often compared with
             Mao Tse-Tung,
               the first Ming Emperor, 1368,
was also a charismatic bandit leader
                  who spiraled off his rocker.
In 1950, historian and deputy mayor of Peking,
                  Wu Han, unwisely,
wrote that early Ming history
             as Mao was sinking into paranoia.
Wu Han died in prison in 1969
            for criticizing the current government
by writing about the past.

*   *   *

Artist and human rights advocate
                    Ai Wei Wei was tortured for 81 days
for investigating the "tofu-dreg schools"
                    that collapsed in the Sichuan earthquake
of 2008.
                    While trying to testify to the slipshod construction,
                                        he was beaten
by police in Chengdu
                    and required emergency surgery
                                        for a cerebral hemorrhage.
Nonetheless, he published a list
                    of 5,385 students killed in the quake.
The great proletariat struggle
                              is now dead
                    in the middle of an industrial revolution,
an expanding consumer economy
                    that ships boatloads of third-rate products
to Walmart and Home Depot.
                    With all the factories and imported cars,
the air in Beijing is so saturated with particulate
                                        you cannot see
                                        five feet
in front of you,
                    let alone to the night stars
                              from which we all arrived.
The men at the top
                    press the automatic window buttons
                              closing out the grainy view
as they're driven

in their Party-provided Buick Regals.
                              They could run successfully
for Congress as Republicans
          not opposed to oil, fracking, or commercial redevelopment.

     *   *   *

There's a line that loops back
                    to Wu Han
                              from the 1960s and Vietnam
                                        via M*A*S*H,
a TV show about a mobile army surgical hospital
                                        during the Korean War.
Everyone knew the subject was Vietnam,
                              the war's human and political failure,
but given the hawkish mood of the nation then,
                    (Let's round up all those hippies,
drop them in the jungle with their peace pamphlets,
                                        and see how they do!)
 you couldn't get backing
                    for a show about the Vietnam war.
                              No, it had to be
dressed up in a Korean time-warp
                    with movie stars and laugh tracks
to insinuate any political critique....
                    Robert McNamara, prime architect of the war,
fell out
          with Johnson and the Joint Chiefs
                    for advising freezing troop levels, a cessation
of bombing in the north,
          handing the ground fighting back to South Vietnam.
In '67 LBJ forced McNamara to resign,

but in '68 Johnson bailed,
leaving the bodies
on the ground, leaving the door open for Nixon, who,
emphasizing a good economy
and successes in foreign affairs—(establishing relations with China)—
won
a landslide re-election in 1972, despite four more years of war.
We were not
bombing Cambodia,
he was not a crook....
58,000+ died, just on our side—
mostly boys
born after WWII, 18-year-olds fresh from high school or replacing
tires and shocks at SEARS,
driving tractors through corn or alfalfa fields—kids
who went surfing
and dropped out of City College ...
the body count announced
each evening on the news
after the RBIs on the sports report.

*   *   *

When it ended, we thought we'd come out on top, but it was another
swing and a miss, the CEOs circling the bases with appreciating
portfolios from Grumman, Boeing, General Dynamics, Standard Oil,
McDonnell Douglas, Pratt & Whitney, Colt Manufacturing, Bank of
America ... you name it.... Same ballgame, they just kept changing
the pitchers.

Now, we all have haircuts,
Hondas, mutual funds—

those of us, that is, whose
pensions were not scooped up by corporate raiders,
"private equity restructuring,"
and international takeovers.
No one's bothered now
by offshore banking,
tax loopholes, the military GNP, and corporate welfare?
Where did we go?
Way past the halfway mark here,
the only community thought arrives
in direct-mail circulars for Assisted Living....
What will there be left
to say for ourselves
with war our only legacy
before we return to particles,
to the irrefutable history of dust?

Christopher Buckley

On Time

> *... non in tempore sed cum tempore Deus creavit ordinem mundi.*
> —St. Augustine

The light years
        arriving after untold time,
                or driving away from us,
the distances lost in it....
        You lie here at night,
                saline drip-
in-the-blood-time,
        star-drift, cloud-drift,
              slowing the gazing
down to waves or packets.
        It's all the same imperceptible time
where you can't see your way
        clear until
           you are somewhere else
looking back,
      say, to 1968, the Chambers Brothers
             enunciating
the obvious
      you were oblivious to,
        Time has come today: Pleiku,
the Pueblo, Tet Offensive, My Lai,
           Russian tanks in Prague,
King, Kennedy,
      Apollo 8 orbiting the moon....

Yet no appreciable change
        in the air around you—
             time-traveling,

the cerebral storeroom,
                    the congealed unlikely jelly where
historical bits
              and pieces coalesce
                          for the time being....
Freight train time, the red shift
                          and whistle of every bright thing
moving away
              from us toward the finite weight of everything
or the timeless weight
                of the infinite—
                          not that long
to make up your mind....

                    For instance, the grey weight of my cat
each night
            settling-on-my-chest time
                          as we breathe together,
the string, the inevitable
                length and portion of time neither of us see
though I have more
              access to the timeless abstractions than she....

Einstein timing out despite his atomic appreciation of the
                                        variables—
the spindrift
            comet trails of chalk across blackboards,
                          the star-white
aurora of his hair—late emblems, ephemera
                          of hours spent revealing
a theory about space,

and the attendant matter
                              of time as well.

My cardiologist slipping the threads through to
                              the ventricle
to keep time a while longer.
                    Bored-stiff-in-the-bones time,
school bell later each day
                    at the end of science-class time—
                                        3:00
at Our Lady of Mt. Carmel School,
                    1958,
                              in the outer precincts
of a flung arm of an average galaxy
                    spinning clockwise somewhere—
the grammar and gravel of it then,
                    the seemingly unending duration
of it—precious monotony now....

Fossil fuel-buried-time that moves
                    us faster
                              around the planet
to our ends.
          Likewise, ice ages, the unlocking
                              of glacial time
melting away,
          everything running out and
                              the fire next time....
Everything takes time.

          Part and parcel,

         thought particles stalling
like Zeno's arrow,
    motionless in theory,
        in flight.... Yet the air
of the Himalayas
    continuing to rise, drifting off
        to the dark edge
where there is no longer
    any of it ... where time dissolves
perhaps?
    The source of it un-sourced,
        bright un-mined ore of it,
the un-enriched absence
    of atomic structure in 96% of whatever it is
that is un-shining out there,
    all that's beyond parsing in the dark.

What then about the instants, the pools
    where we set forth,
the open locks and flood gates,
    the unmetaphysical eons where
salt encrypted our blood,
    where every paper boat
        and soul set forth
with the invisible
    ink of time
    imprinted on each cell?
        What we have then
is the brief
    bread-crumb equivalent of time
        across the cosmic expanse,

the here
      and available now,
            the whisper and hum of it,
                  microwaves
chorusing in the rocks—
          the gravity and attenuated driving
                dead-end
finally unendurable force of it.
           Just our glint of time
               in time, time....

Parallel Universes

Recent research has indicated the possibility of the gravitational pull of other universes on ours.
　　　　—Wikipedia

Einstein didn't live long enough
to work out the Theory of Everything,
the exact mileage to the immense ...
but if parallel universes are the case,
he's out there in the stars still
putting the pieces together
even though Max Planck's study
of radiation suggested divergent laws
operating beneath the floorboards
of gravity and light....
　　　　　　　　　　Now
they've turned up *cosmic bruises*—
4 circular patterns in the microwave
background radiation—evidence
that our universe has crashed
into others.... One soap bubble
rubs against another and
you have a foam of universes,
a mathematical crash and run-out
to the other side of the end of anything
you now have on hand ... almost
endless permutations until you arrive
at a duplicate of our own
"Goldilocks zone" habitable planet!?
More or less.
　　　　　　It could vary by a micron
or two—the tiniest sub-atomic backfire

or jitter of an electron or quark
and scads of different outcomes,
though cosmic strings vibrate
essentially as Parmenides set it down
in his poem about the music of the spheres,
leaving out the north star as the still point
of the turning earth of course....
                                    Thus
Elvis is still doing TV Spectaculars
from Hawaii; Al Gore was re-elected,
Rick got on that plane with Ilsa,
everyone in the middle east is sharing
pita bread and baba ganoush with his neighbor,
and somewhere on a stage Burns & Allen
are taking a bow: *Say Goodnight, Gracie!*
There's an even chance that communism
did not collapse, and instead of making reservations
at that French/Bulgarian fusion bistro,
you're eyeing the two potatoes and shriveled bit
of beet root left in the shop—some guy selling
lamp shades out the back....
                            Sergei Krikalev,
Russian cosmonaut who flew six space missions,
could well head transportation for the EU.
We're here on condition that everything occurs
within the parenthesis of time,
within the end-stopped tributaries
to a sea, a great blind quantum scramble
where we arrive too late to the table
to translate the oscillating patterns and
packets of light.

With every veneration
of my breath my cells are imminently obliged
to oblivion. You choose one god
or another, but religion is a trial,
an excuse to feel good about the fact
that you might be dead soon,
that, before you know it,
all your atoms will be headed
somewhere without you.

Christopher Buckley

Qualitative, Non-linear Differential Equations

As far as the laws of mathematics refer to reality, they are not certain; and as far as they are certain, they do not refer to reality.
—Albert Einstein

*in a dazzle of splendid
approximations*
— Philip Levine

Until 1700, *mathematics* commonly meant
astrology ... first cousin to soothsaying,
to augurs who offered divination
by interpreting the flight of birds,
the entrails of owls.
                    Despite all
the math courses I was subjected to,
I may well have had a clearer view
to solving problems in my life
by charting Saturn setting in my house
of finance or deciphering hexagrams of the *I Ching*
than trying to work out the moshpit
of letters, signs, and numbers in equations
and set theory.
                    Early on, I was lost
in long division which took me
longer than most students in the room.
Then came the labyrinthine and baffling
processes, the cryptic calculations,
axiomatic and impenetrable formulae—
sines, cosines and every tangential wonder
said to provide insight to, or predictions about,
our nature ... all of it absolutely beyond
my comprehension, light-years past

the *one-potato, two-potato, three-potato, four*
bedrock of my numerical acumen.
                                        The only
thing that stayed with me—besides the correct
spelling of A-R-I-T-H-M-E-T-I-C from the memory aid
A rat in the house may eat the ice cream—
was the phrase, *Qualitative, Nonlinear*
Differential Equation. This jumbled mouthful
tumbled out with assonance, a credible rhythm,
though the only thing I came away with
was a subtextual proximity to theology,
a connotative refutation of much
of the doctrine on the main menu
in Catholic school.
                        An introduction to a text
on differential equations discovered on-line
warns: *"Analytical solutions cannot, in general,*
be found, cannot be written out. We may make
numerical approximations, however in most
applications **solutions may be unavailable.** *"*
Nothing there I didn't already know
from years of Algebra, Geometry and Trig,
from the incunabula of belief. It concluded:
"Even though numerical solutions suggest
certain properties, they are only valid
for limited solutions on finite intervals,
and therefore cannot be used to determine
the qualitative properties of all solutions
to the original equation."
                            That was it,
"the original equation"—Aquinas' medieval

First Cause/prime mover arguments
for intelligent design were clearly undermined,
especially in light of parallel universes,
the final computations for eleven-dimensional
strings, and confirmation of the Higgs boson
God Particle, not to mention the black
holes at the center of every galaxy
eating up time and matter like there's
no tomorrow, questioning how the cosmic
bank shots were called in the first place?
Top that with the fact that, regardless
of all the efforts made, the earth will
end up fried, crispier than a papadum
in the reconstituted oil of time—so how then
will all the paradisical platforms and
our celestially stored and glorified souls
orbit above the defeated skies
one well may ask?
                    I wrote to my pal
from 2nd grade at Our Lady of Mount Carmel
who could do fractions and long division
like nobody's business, who now teaches
math at an eastern state university,
and he explained: "'Non-linear' means
it's modeling something that is changing
exponentially. 'Qualitative' means
you're not going to get a point answer
but will have an indication of the quality
of the range of answers you do get.
Differential equations are used to model
everything from bridge building

to quantum interactions
to economics."
        Still a bit impenetrable
unless you speak high math or never developed
any misgivings about faith? I began to think
about the guys who built the San Francisco-
Oakland Bay Bridge, about the interstate
bridges collapsing on the evening news
over the last several years—who believed in
and hired the engineers? And I read about
the Black-Scholes Partial Differential Equation
that won the Nobel Prize for Economics
in 1997 and was the impetus for the entire
derivatives market, which crashed spectacularly ...
and realized that if Bush and the neocons
had succeeded in putting Social Security
into the stock market, there'd be a lot of us now
living *under* bridges....
        Neils Bohr
made the calculation of energy levels
in stationary orbits of electrons, postulating
that the emission of light happens when
an electron moves into a lower orbit ...
and Rutherford figured out that most
of an atom is empty space, and therefore
I wonder what percentage, if any, of that
might be the soul, and what all the atomic bits
add up to when it comes to that
                                 orchestral
and chaotic whirling, the bumper cars, and
pinball probability of particle physics?

We either subscribe to a cosmic motherboard
and inter-stellar IT stage directions
working out predictably enough that
we can adjust to the one thing we do know
is certain other than taxes, or, we accept
it all has next to nothing to do with us
once we hit the EXIT, shuffle off this mortal coil....
You can't, of course, prove anything
one way or the other, but for deductive
purposes it seems likely that first-hand evaluation
at street level will prove more accurate,
specific, and useful than a hat full
of theoretical equations, but what
do I know?
     I know the stars are
grinding down more or less imperceptibly,
like the attrition of our cells, our bones
more noticeably. So, as gravity has its way
with us and we grow shorter over time
and face the attenuated dead-ends
of most hypotheses, mathematical or
religious—like the figures of saints
rising on the clouds behind the altar
in the churches of our youth—there is
next to nothing to support any of it.
Hymns, incense, some smoke lifting
on sunlight through the high transoms ...
dark energy holding the spiral arms
of galaxies together, every mystical
concoction and bit of spiritual backlighting
that, like a metaphysical Ponzi scheme,

all promise continuation in one form
or another when we're done—and
more where that came from.

for Tuck Schneider

Cosmology: at the End of Sterns' Wharf

Behind me,
a few house lights
blink in the hills
underscoring the last
early morning stars ...
a blue cloud falls
into the amnesia
of the sea.
The stars dissolve,
and it appears
that there's nothing
holding us in place
against the unmoving
dark?
          For a minute
I see an outline, a bit
of tailor's chalk marking
the indigo sky,
but it all dissipates
with the breeze spinning
up west to east,
the earth turning
so slowly it seems,
it's hard to believe....

The sky bleaches out
and there's nothing to do
with the disobliging heavens,
the fact that each night
starlight spells out
our irrelevance

at a distance that more
and more I am coming to
comprehend....
            How many
outcomes enter the mind,
besides the old one—
silence out there
from here to the unknown
edge? The least pinpoint
of light burns across the brain,
and we have no choice
but to wonder where
it comes from,
given the assumption
that we are heading for it
in some form
at some point,
outside of time....

The little bit of it
I have left I waste
looking out beyond
the uneasiness rising
through my legs
to my fingertips—
an abstract pain,
some seed of light
inaccessible as ever.

And still sometimes
on the horizon, I see

a Phoenician sail
coming into view around
the point, bringing us
grape vines and an alphabet
not all that long ago....

We have spent billions
wondering how many planets
have a trace of water,
and each time
we get back an answer
that suggests we've been
abandoned here,
by someone,
by infinitesimal chance,
by some mitochondrial
roll of interstellar dice....

The sea is quiet ...
I no longer know
what I want to hear—
either way, I find
myself shifting from one
foot to the other,
not a leg to stand on.

III

New Science, Etymology, & the Ineffable

In memoriam: William Matthews

My wife tells me that in thinking of all that might be
out there, seen and unseen, our brains comprehend
as much about the universe as our cats, Cecil and Lizzie,
do of the world outside our fenced yard where they are
never allowed to go ... e.g., multiverses, p-branes,
M-theory, 11-dimensional superstrings, red-shifted galaxies
taking the A train toward the Great Attractor, and
ad infinitum re the pre-masticated cosmology books
I read before I turn the lamp out and drift off to sleep—
in short, every new, salient, and expansive fact or supposition
I unearth of the unqualifiable cosmos with the support
of some Sauvignon blanc poured over a moon-white
ice cube or two, just to start....
                                        I remember
the nuns in grammar school telling a handful of us
in back that we weren't going anywhere
if we couldn't get the new Set-Theory algebra
they'd just unloaded on us, that such indolence
as ours would send us straight to hell. And thus
our poor thick heads were hammered with intangible
equations to get us graduated and out the door,
where we'd be someone else's problem,
floating in our dull orbits a city or two away,
which, in the '50s, might as well have been light years,
a year itself a longer string of time than any of us
could fully imagine. I just sat there looking out
the huge windows at the sky spun above the acacia trees,
knowing that I preferred the unexamined
and intuitive efforts of the clouds to anything

arithmetical.

       50 years later, and no one's calculated
where all that time has gone, except perhaps Einstein,
and reports say he didn't like writing out the math
and showing his work any more than the rest of us;
he just worked most of it out in his head. His notion
of curved space-time circling back on us, might well
explain the big invisible picture, but it also sounds
vaguely religious. I think of the clouds just continuing
around the earth, *continuing* being the operative word.
Yet Einstein's idea does extrapolate Supergravity,
and that clarifies how the energy of a large number
of particles curves the universe, forms a bound state,
like a black hole, inside which, they say, time
comes to an end. But let's not go there.

                    My cats,
in their comfortable middle age are content lying
on the wide, cool, afternoon lawn, content with
the lizards some finite force has darting occasionally
before them in the light; they no longer give a thought
to the wire mesh along the fence-top that holds them
here. I look out at night, at what I once described
as the barbed-wire of stars, but there's no limit now
and that guess does not fill in any blanks. I love
that wonderful photo of Einstein riding a bicycle
around his driveway in Princeton; he's wearing
a cardigan, and tie, shoes shined, and he's sockless,
grinning for all he's worth, having just escaped
(I still remember the feeling) from school into
the freedom of the afternoon air.

                     It's difficult

to travel anywhere these days since we have the cats.
They depend on us for a reliable interpretation of experience
and a variety of cuisine. My wife says she just hopes
we can get back to Europe one day, now that we can
finally afford that gondola ride in Venice—that black hole
of tourist budgets. A little travel, one hopeful dimension
that appears to be *effable* re our remaining years,
(a word that is only part of a word sliding down the time-line,
Latin to Old French to Middle English, a verb we should—
in a perfect world—be able to use, as our friend Bill liked to pun)
whereas all beyond here is dark and *ineffable,* tied inescapably
to every last thing we will never be sure about.

The Theory of Everything—Science, Religion, Grammar School, Surfing, & the 99¢ Store

Einstein didn't worry about his socks, attending temple, or his soul;
he played violin in the kitchen and worked out the math in his head,
trying to put gravity, electromagnetism, the weak and strong
nuclear forces back together again.
                              In 1929, fishing for scientific
A-list backup, and counting on the famous statement about
            physics—
God does not play dice with the universe—a rabbi telegraphed Einstein
to ask if he believed in God. Einstein replied, "I believe in Spinoza's God
who reveals himself in the orderly harmony of what exists, not in a God
who concerns himself with the fates and actions of human beings."
Game over.
            Mid-'50s, Catholic grammar school, and no one interested
in explaining just what invisible force held our atoms together;
rather, we were daily indoctrinated with the likelihood that most of us
would be roasting for *All Eternity* on a fiery spit. The nuns and priests
were sure they knew what was what, sure that you needed to give up
everything on earth to wear a starry crown and walk the streets of
            Paradise
alongside the saints.
                  But even before I cracked my General Science text,
I had my doubts ... walking on water, rising from the dead ...
a snowball's chance in hell, I thought—it was all a spiritual
            shakedown,
a boondoggle, a glorified Madison Ave. marketing campaign for Faith.
Everyone was just making things up—no one could diagram
the unseen syntax of the stars—the implied subject, the indirect
objects—any more than they could fly to the moon.

*   *   *

But by then it was too late to cross our fingers and call "King's X"
or "Time out," as we did when the light spun slowly out of the tops
of eucalyptus in the west and we were called in from play,
each of our particles vibrating in its own atomic membrane,
though we were sure it was our own hand in front of our face
and not a slate of molecules taken on contingency. Nonetheless,
we hoped there might be something inside every buzzing electron
smashing away inside the cyclotron of our blood system—light
zooming out our skin and eyes for at least as long as we were young
      . . .
and all the while every last illuminated, dark, or blazing bit of matter
was speeding away from us through space, redshifted toward a blind,
unknowable edge regardless of what was proclaimed joyfully
in choirs beneath an indeterminate sky, where we knew
there had to be a catch, something scribbled on the undersides
of passing clouds, something vague and weary as the waves
sliding into shore, their equivocal code unread inside the surf....

Beneath it all, I borrowed a body from time, traveled curl and froth,
living on little more than gravity, sea-winds, and tides, which came to
about as much finally as what St. Theresa the Little Flower had,
who ate nothing but light, who rose into the ecstasies of air—
which, had I thought it over, might have half-way made sense
as I rode the nose of my board, screaming down a thin section
above the rocks at Miramar Point, hands thrown up in hosannas
to a secular sky, kinetic in my bones and skin, never taking a second
to bless the electrons that sparked and networked invisibly
from my tendons to the lip of the wave, everything shot through
with salt and un-seeable space—as were my briny synapses,

the cartload of electricity within the flex coils and strings
of my corpuscles, in the apparently inexhaustible fabric of my breath.

Every 50 years the smart guys think they've made the final calculations,
have a system to count the cosmic cards before the lights go out.
Even as a child the stars represented everything, or a least a good
portion of it in the schematics of hope as each day we let it all ride,
double or nothing, minute to minute on life everlasting.

   * * *

And yesterday, checking out at the 99¢ Store—where I go to save
on vegetables, yogurt, paper towels, crunchies for my cat, most
everything under the sun—I pushed my cart along the aisle
of school supplies and picked up a copy of the *TIME/LIFE*
publication, *100 Ideas That Changed the World,* resting on top
of the remaindered books—a magazine-size paperback
with photos of Einstein, a computer keyboard, an artist's
depiction of the Big Bang, and a Greek Orthodox mosaic of Jesus
blessing us all from its glossy cover. The clerk, who I know
from my weekly visits, is a Mexican woman, older even than me,
white hair, soft grey eyes, someone who shouldn't be working
any more. As she scans my items she stops and looks at the book,
points to the photo of Einstein, and asks me if he isn't that old guy
from *Chico and the Man?* You remember that TV series,
don't you? Freddie Prinze? And I say Yes, yes, mid '70s,
I saw some episodes long ago … but this photo's of a scientist,
Albert Einstein, not Jack Albert who played the owner of the garage
in that East L.A. neighborhood. *Einstein* draws a blank for her.
Sure looks like that *viejo* on TV, she says … then looks at me,
shakes her head a little and sighs, "Where does the time go?"

Relativity

> ... people went in ... got crushed to infinite density and disappeared. That was the traditional view ... however, Stephen Hawking stunned the world by showing that black holes would leak particles and radiation, and in fact eventually explode, although for a hole the mass of a star it would take longer than the age of the universe.
> —"A Black Hole Mystery Wrapped in a Firewall Paradox," Aug. 12, 2013, *The New York Times,* Dennis Overbye

Now, if you jump into a black hole—
        that trapdoor in space gulping down
matter, energy,
    and gobs of interstellar light
        like there's no tomorrow—
you're presented with a choice
    between being crushed traditionally
by unimaginable gravity, or—
    according to recent computations—
being flash-fried
    by a firewall of energy
        faster than a Mars Bar
at a county fair....
    It turns out black holes are the extrapolated end
of Einstein's theory
    where matter and energy warp
        every speck of space
and time—
    the standard example of a bowling ball
        rolling around
on a trampoline still obtains.
    Too big a bowling ball—
        too much matter
and energy in one place—

and the fabric of space sinks
so thoroughly
into itself that the density becomes infinite …
and it's lights out
all around.
But really, who's going there?
Or anywhere, finally?
which looks to be
the more pressing question
on our collective plate.
Either way,
a ton of bricks
remains a ton of bricks
for every purpose
on earth,
and it feels like we have all the gravity
we need—
especially with every bit
of space debris ready to rain back down
on our heads....
In 1916,
when his equations were shown
to result in black holes,
Einstein thought it was absurd.
Nevertheless,
these gravitational beasts pulse
at the hearts of most galaxies, and
millions and billions of times
more massive than the sun,
these invisible
leftovers

of a dead star's collapse,

                     polka-dot space

like sprinkles on your Dunkin' Donut ...

                the math adds up.

I've read—though I can't begin

            to work out the field calculations—

that your GPS depends on general relativity

         to keep time

as you move about,

       but even it can't help you

          in a black hole

where every bit of matter's

        lost in the cosmic compactor, or

is nuked by the new thinking /

      that firewall of energy....

One deep,

   unassailable theory

       and still so many numbers

to crunch before

     they think they know, for sure,

          again....

But no matter ...

    when you stop to think about it,

to figure it out,

   we have all the time in the world....

Deep Time

> *Consider the Earth's history as the old measure of the English yard, the distance from the King's nose to the tip of his outstretched hand. One stroke of a nail file on his middle finger erases human history.*
> —John McPhee

It's not certain
that the stars are still there,
lagging behind their light....

Over a dark sea,
a boat drifts on the outskirts
toward Tierra del Fuego,
or stalls, perhaps,
in the horse latitudes ...
but the horses running through
your dreams, who knows
where they belong?

Despite all the instructions
your mother left,
you know next to nothing—
just the clouds for comfort
as you sift through
the small brown photographs,
look out the window to a grey
shipwrecked horizon....

Some black-&-white reels
replay the '40s in a backwater
where your father stepped out
for a smoke and gazed above

street lights, the band taking five
somewhere outside Chillicothe.
You might as well look for him
by the cloakroom, or in the alley,
and no matter who you bump into,
turn around and walk away
as the last of autumn etches the air
a month or two before you arrive
out of nowhere—he never saw it coming....
Keep going through the stoplight
blinking at the corner ...
it will make no difference
in the long run
if you don't turn back—
he will hardly ever be there
anyway.
              Particles or waves,
it all disappears, as far as you
can see. Tonight, these are not
the icy tresses of angels
hovering above the cliffs,
only the immediate
reciprocation of leaves,
the bite of salt air,
the blue strata of evening
dissolving to ash ...
what little you're left
to remember as the flashes
of light, the seconds,
gradually clear your mind.

Beneath the Clouds–On Borrowed Time

You're living the cliché—
barely a moment
for the thin grace
of altocumulus,
white and liturgical,
or dull as the sand
at high tide....
Not half a chance
to re-read the fine print
that doesn't extend
the warranty, the life-line ...
actuaries, in their grey
monks' robes having calculated
the return on coverage,
down to each unseen
quark or muon,
our every associated iota
which will be called back
to rattle around
in who knows what
portion of the black
can of creation ...
the universe racing—
by our latest count—
for close to14 billions years
to pull itself apart
somewhere else....

Like a child walking
through long museum halls,
the faces of your family

pass from sight, gone
with the great masters
into the high self-portraits
hung in the halls of clouds,
held then only in mists
rising through the loose
atmosphere of the mind....

As for the nebulous
swirl of the Aurora Borealis
at the edge of our air,
most of the time
it's barely visible
to the naked eye,
yet now and then bright enough
to read a newspaper by
at night. It's not a dance
of the spirits
as the Cree had it,
nor a sign from God
as medieval Europeans
believed ... the slow
shimmering geomagnetic
waves barely interrupt
the radio which no one
listens to anymore....
Crosswind, starched-white streets
of cumulus, razor blade
of light at the horizon
and you have your blank map
tossed out again on the blue.

Add some altostratus, thin
inscriptions, un-translatable
as ever....
          Cross the sticks
and stones of childhood
off your list, cross off middle age ...
and even if you can still hear
Ben Webster's "Time on My Hands,"
you only have ghosted exhalations,
the wispy striations
like beamed notes
on the fading sheet music
of the sky. Here you are,
where nothing returns
beyond the insubstantial
gratuities of light,
the capriccios of wind,
nothing beyond white caps
whipped up and gone,
marking the lost way out ...
a low marine layer hugging
the coast, lining the road
ahead, a reflection
of our fears undisguised,
and you haven't got a prayer.

Stars

... they are the endlessness of our longing to grasp things.
     —Nazim Hikmet

Tonight, looking at the stars, I realize I've already arrived
at what my life was coming to ... plenty of space out there,
just over 4% of everything glimmering in the emptiness....
I never saw myself riding down the Champs-Elysées
beside Sasha Distell or Charles Aznavour, one or the other
of them humming "Stardust" or "La Vie en Rose." Rather,
it took place mostly in a grey suburban light that reaches back
through mid-century where memory reruns in black & white,
where I can still see Rosemary Clooney on TV singing, *Hey there,
you with the stars in your eyes....*
                             I vaguely remember running
off a street corner somewhere in 1950, into the blinding sun—
Hudsons, Nash Ramblers, Fords, and Studebakers flying by.
It could have been Springfield, MO, Charleston, WV,
or Columbus, OH? My legs were sturdy and I was going as fast
as they'd carry me in any direction, but my father was there
to pull on my harness and hold me suspended in space,
a foot or so away from the traffic barreling through
the yellow signal light.
                       I was happy, knew no more
of life and death there—the red star of my hand held up
to shield my eyes—than I knew of the 11 dimensions
of string theory I'd wonder about 60 years later when I was
trying to figure where it all invisibly goes, a bit after the fact.
Not that long a time when you've lived it already ...
everyone in your family gone, quickly as all the stars
disappearing each dawn.

*   *   *

Stars again above the deepening blue ... so many meanings
carried the distance of the mind—our lives by association
with light, wherever it comes from.... So little time
to sit here looking out beyond the doubt that rises daily
beneath our feet, that flags down the abstract scattershot
of hope the heart holds on to.
         If the gods left a message
for us, it's in the dust, in salt dried across the rocks,
in the wind raising objections as far back as you can go.
Pythagoras and Aristotle agreed that stars whirl around
the earth—Pythagoras hearing a tangential music
of the spheres fixing them in place, Aristotle seeing angels
pushing the celestial orbs across crystal tracks....
And with Copernicus redrawing the vast order and spins,
the floodgates opened to even wider speculation. Now,
theoretical physicists say everything depends on the vibration
of strings in 11 dimensions, though it's all invisible
as it ever was.
         Something called Wilkinson Microwave
Anistropy Probe has measured the remnant radiant heat
from the Big Bang via background radiation, and it pretty much
confirms that the universe goes on forever....
         99 years ago
Einstein's special theory proposed that there is no absolute
time or space—rather it's one thing—each bright bit having
its side effect, the proverbial bowling ball bounced on the fabric
of the celestial trampoline.
         Yet little's changed—and it's nothing
compared to the discovery of penicillin, the invention of the

      airplane,
telephone, or automobile. So what do the stars add up to
as far as we're concerned?
                       Francis Bacon, who roughed out
inductive reasoning, and so was the star of the scientific method,
believed in God, but believed equally in reason, and was devoted to
collecting evidence based on observation. He died of pneumonia
contracted testing cold as a preservative—out on a starless night,
stuffing a chicken with snow. Such are our shining rewards.

After a Winter Storm: Grand Unified Field Theory

Out here, on the point, I think
                    I see as much as I'm ever going to ...
spindrift splashed in air,
             time and space dissolving
                       down storm tracks
to the east....
        The rummage of clouds
                sloughing stale gusts,
the fogs of industry,
          and our sky's still stuffed
                  with afterthoughts
from the Greeks—
        Leucippus and Democritus
                working out
that it's only atoms so far
        as we're concerned,
              along with the four
split forces that account for us,
        for every molecule
             or cathedral
we turn up.
        Kelp, clam shells, driftwood
              from the south seas ...
bits and pieces,
        nothing you can do
            about the deep
clock of the universe
        slip-streamed on starlight,
                unwinding,
but never slowing down—
        every shining thing redshifted,

                                 whizzing
past our ears
        as we place a provisional penny
                        on this collection plate
of dust....
        Add every zero you can,
                  we still end up
with just the fine powder
           of the past in our hands....
                        Who knows
how the ionosphere developed
            into a backboard
                  for radio waves?
Programs your father punched in
            on the chrome buttons
in that Pontiac 60 years ago
           bounced around and are still heading out—
Gunsmoke, The Whistler, Mr. & Mrs. North—
                  zooming past
the cosmic street lamps,
        the only interruption a voice
                      instructing
listeners to *Call for Philip Morris*....
           A sky's wind-ripped edge is all
the evidence of our breath,
        returning to what exactly—
solar dust on the sea?
        And the sea is dull
              as that zinc counter
in the neighborhood bar,
        one thing I could count on besides

a Fernet Branca,
                    those dark wings spreading inside me despite
the bitter cold ...
                    a place for apostates,
                              home-spun astrophysicists
to gather for a smoke, a glass
                    of groundless speculation.
                                        Wise Up!
a good salt air slap in the face says,
                    even gravity's ignored
by the sleepwalking clouds.
              I can still hear the thunder rolling
from the back room,
                    someone breaking 9-ball ...
                              fat chance the 1
and 2 sink in opposite corners,
              the 3 and 4 in the sides at the same time....
I'm wondering where, amid all the quantum mechanics,
                              a soul turns up
in a garage full of theoretical parts—
                    lost among more dust drifting
across pages of Natural Philosophy
                    from the Middle Ages where
they hadn't the slightest intimation
                    of the eleven dimensions
that might elegantly resolve
              the old equation.
                    Electromagnetic, weak or
strong nuclear forces,
              the circumstantial evidence
                         of gravity—

                                        the idea is
that they can one day seamlessly be thrown
                            back together
like evening light gathering itself
                    across the bay....
                                Still, almost
everything we can put our finger on
                    bangs along
                                consistently enough,
one charmed quark or left-handed neutrino
                            after another....
Centuries of star gazing
                    and nothing's clear
                                as we still wonder
if we've come this far
                only to come this far?

On the Patio, after Reading Democritus

Nothing exists except atoms and empty space; everything else is opinion.
—Democritus

I pour a little Absolut,
as clear as the glass
that holds it, clear as the soul
which Democritus said
consisted of atoms of fire....
As good a guess as any—
the air long let out of
the old expectations,
that film of atoms
that was said to contain
the characteristics of the gods,
who, like the stars,
were not immortal.

And wafer by wafer
the darkness arrives
on my tongue ...
what was it my father said
back there when I was 7—
the blink of an eye
and it's all behind you?
He was a dour man
who imparted that vision
to a child and was gone,
leaving the irresolute motion
of the sea as guide—
a haze, a veil between me

and whatever point there was
in the wind where chicken hawks
spun upward, lifting themselves
above the spindrift thumbed
from the bay, the tides fumbling
to shore, winter grating,
gravel washing out
at low tide.
        And the islands
floating across the channel,
the music of the spheres
murmuring in the background,
microwave radiation,
its gravity waves
yet to reach us....
          Still,
the stars pile up across the dark,
light years, like the sound
of a sled through snow
lost on the edge of wilderness....

Dog-walkers, star-gazers,
either way there's something
in our thoughts that interprets
the circles of light that fall to us,
that hold our gaze out there
where meteors streak
whether we are watching
with our sleeping hearts, or not—
our dreams tied to some idea

or other about our lives,
some silver stumbling cloud
being drawn into the gullet of time.

What if, finally, there was nothing
to fear?

Notes

CHAOS THEORY:

V. Prime Mover vs. Qualitative Nonlinear Differential Equations

> This is a found poem, taken from the Preface to *A First Course in the Qualitative Theory of Differential Equations;* James Hetao Liu, (Prentice Hall, 2003)

VI. Nothing

> Much of this section is in debt to K.C. Cole's *The Hole In the Universe* (Harcourt, Inc., 2001)

VII. Fractals

> The mathematical roots of the idea of fractals have been traced through a formal path of published works, starting in the 17th century with notions of recursion, then moving through increasingly rigorous mathematical treatment of the concept to the study of continuous but not differentiable functions in the 19th century, and on to the coining of the word *fractal* in the 20th century with a subsequent burgeoning of interest in fractals and computer-based modeling in the 21st century. The term "fractal" was first used by mathematician Benoît Mandelbrot in 1975. Mandelbrot based it on the Latin *fractus* meaning "broken" or "fractured," and used it to extend the concept of theoretical fractional dimensions to geometric patterns in nature.
>
> —Wikipedia

IX. Chaos Thinking

> re: "how everything came from nothing ..."
>
> "The new effect hinges on the behavior of particularly strange particles called neutral B-mesons, which are famous for not being able to make up their minds. They oscillate back and forth trillions of times a second between their regular state and their antimatter state. As it happens, the mesons, created in the proton-antiproton collisions, seem to go from their antimatter state to their mater state more rapidly than they go the other way around, leading to an eventual preponderance of matter over antimatter of about 1 percent, when they decay to muons."
>
> —*The New York Times,* May 17, 2010, Dennis Overbye

XI. God Particle

re: "the scree of math"

A mathematical term used to represent a constant, which isn't constant.

A pile of rubble.

A mass of small loose stones that form or cover a slope on a mountain.

—Urban Dictionary

In an experiment called DZero at the lab's Tevatron particle collider, scientists recently found that collisions of protons and antiprotons produced pairs of matter particles more often than pairs of antimatter particles.

The difference was tiny—less than one percent—but it can't be explained by a standard model that assumes the existence of a single Higgs boson, said study co-author Adam Martin, a theoretical physicist at Fermilab.

—Ken Than, *National Geographic News,* June 16, 2012

Acknowledgments

Alligator Juniper : "On the Patio," "Creed," "Online Facts About the Sun"

Archaeopteryx: "Anthropic Principle"

Askew: "Qualitative, Non-linear Differential Equations"

Hubbub: "Cosmology: at the End of Sterns' Wharf"

Lake Effect: "Stars"

Plume: "Beneath the Clouds—On Borrowed Time," "The Half-life of Revolution—Particle Physics, History, Baseball, & Baby-Boomers," "After a Winter Storm: Grand Unified Field Theory," "On Time," "Parallel Universes"

Rattle: "The Theory of Everything"

Verdad: "Deep Time," "God-Particle Postscript from the Large Hadron Collider"

Zone 3: "Chaos Theory I, II, III, IV, V, VI, VII, VIII, IX, X, XI"

Thanks to *Zone 3* and Blas Falconer for their annual poetry award for *Chaos Theory* in the Spring 2013 issue.

Thanks, as always, to Gary Young, Jon Veinberg and Nadya Brown for support and help with these poems.

ABOUT THE AUTHOR

Christopher Buckley's *Star Journal: Selected Poems* was published by the Univ. of Pittsburgh Press in 2016. *Back Room at the Philosophers' Club*, Buckley's 20th book of poetry (Stephen F. Austin State Univ. Press), won the *Lascaux Review*'s Poetry Book Prize for 2015. SFA Press also published *Varieties of Religious Experience* in 2013. *Rolling The Bones* won the 2009 *Tampa Review* Poetry Prize and was published by the Univ. of Tampa Press in 2010, which published *White Shirt* in 2011.

Buckley was a 2007–2008 Guggenheim Fellow in Poetry. He has been awarded a Fulbright Award in Creative Writing to the former Yugoslavia, four Pushcart Prizes, two awards from the Poetry Society of America, and received NEA grants in poetry for 2001 and 1984.

With Gary Young, Buckley is the editor of *The Geography of Home: California's Poetry of Place* (Hey Day Books, 1999). With David Oliveira and M.L. Williams, he is editor of *How Much Earth: The Fresno Poets* (The Round House Press, 2001). For the Univ. of Michigan Press Under Discussion series, he edited *The Poetry of Philip Levine: Stranger To Nothing*, 1991.

More recently he has edited the poetry anthologies *Bear Flag Republic: Prose Poems & Poetics from California* (with Gary Young) Alcatraz Editions, 2008; *Homage To Vallejo*, Greenhouse Review Press, 2006. With Alexander Long, he edited *A Condition of the Spirit: The Life and Work of Larry Levis* (Eastern Washington Univ. Press, 2004); with Christopher Howell, *Aspects of Robinson: Homage to Weldon Kees* (The Backwaters Press, 2011); again co-edited with Gary Young, *One for the Money: the Sentence as a Poetic Form* (Lynx House Press, 2012); and with Jon Veinberg, *Messenger to the Stars: A Luis Omar Salinas New Selected Poems & Reader* (Tebot Bach, 2014).

Over the last 40 years his poetry has appeared in *APR, Poetry, FIELD, The Georgia Review, The Iowa Review, TriQuarterly, The Kenyon Review, Ploughshares, The New Yorker, The Nation, The Hudson Review, The Gettysburg Review, Quarterly West, Prairie Schooner, The Southern Review, Five Points, The Harvard Review, & New Letters*.